FROM NOW ON

Nerise Howes

iUniverse, Inc.
Bloomington

FROM NOW ON

iUniverse books may be ordered through booksellers or by contacting:

iUniverse
1663 Liberty Drive
Bloomington, IN 47403
www.iuniverse.com
1-800-Authors (1-800-288-4677)

Because of the dynamic nature of the Internet, any Web addresses or links contained in this book may have changed since publication and may no longer be valid.

ISBN: 978-1-4502-7769-3 (sc)
ISBN: 978-1-4502-7771-6 (ebk)

Printed in the United States of America

iUniverse rev. date: 12/28/2010

FROM NOW ON...

I dedicate this workbook to my beloved husband Duncan, my beautiful daughter Leotie, to my mum Elaine, my dad Henry and to my sisters Claire and Sylvie. Also, to my extended family and to all my lovely friends who have come into my life to help me change and grow. Thank you.

Contents

Introduction

I never actually planned on writing this book. One seemingly insignificant morning, I awoke with a strong and strange desire to write something down … what it was I did not know. Trusting this strange impulse I went with the flow of the unknown and found myself writing down the very first line of the book … Hello Most Beautiful Soul. Surprised and intrigued by these words, I decided to continue writing. Was I recalling a dream? Where did this inspiration come from? Was I talking to myself? What was the purpose of this exercise? The answers to these questions became insignificant as I continued to write. It became clear to me that I was being guided to put this workbook together.

I studied psychotherapy, life coaching, and various healing modalities. Having explored many different spiritual and esoteric teachings throughout my life, I have actively worked with the chakras or energy centres, and running workshops as a teacher of Chakradance in Australia.

So taking all this into account, I believe it allowed for a communication to occur that could be translated, viewed and channelled through and from within these associated mediums or modalities. Since writing this workbook I became inspired to continue my studies in the Metaphysical field and have completed a Doctor of Metaphysical Counselling at the Metaphysical University of Sedona in the USA.

Most of the practical exercises you will find in this book have been structured within and around the functioning of the seven main chakras or energy centres.

It became quite clear to me that this book was to be written with the view of simplicity and practicality. It is not an intellectually challenging book that provides a lot of theoretical knowledge. Much of what you read you will, no doubt, have heard before in some form or variation. This book provides a space from within a structured plan, to explore the self through various practical exercises. Each exercise is intended to bring awareness physically, mentally, emotionally and spiritually.

I have found that the greatest insight into self and beyond sometimes comes from the simplest form or process, and I am constantly reminded of this truth.

We each have a very specific part to play in the greater scheme of things ... we simply need to remember what it is. This is part of the message of the book - to constantly keep reminding us that what is important in this life is our intention behind our actions. We need to start putting into practice what we theoretically know of how to effectively live in this world. The best way to integrate this is to start applying practical principles within the realm of our daily lives.

As a fellow traveller on a journey of self-discovery, I wish you, the reader and finder of this book, blessings of love and inspiration. May whatever you seek be found and may you come to the realisation that you have a very unique part to play, here in this life and beyond.

My deepest gratitude to the loving being or energy, who guided me to create this workbook.

I hope you enjoy the journey.
Warmly,
Nerise

Hello Most Beautiful Soul,

At last we meet again. It is no coincidence that you have found this book. This book has found *you*! Life works in strange and mysterious ways. I have been waiting for this perfect place in time; now you are ready, ready to embark upon a journey … a journey deep into *yourself*. Please remember that you will not be alone, for we will be journeying together. I shall be a witness, a friend, a confidant. Together we will laugh, cry and wonder at the beauty of this strange and mysterious life … *your* life … for this book is all about *you*. This book will be your mirror.

May I add, that it is an honour to meet again, for we have always known each other since the beginning of time. Who am I? This does not matter at present. But curious as you are, be patient, I shall reveal myself to you in many ways. You have a very special part to play in this world. Do not underestimate your significance in the greater scheme of things; I am simply here to help you remember. To remind you that you are a being of great beauty and light! In time you will come to see this for yourself, but first things first.

What is required of you is your commitment and courage; as well as your honesty and good humour. If you are willing to join me on this journey, then let us begin.

Write your name here_____

Now, say your name out loud as if you have just been introduced to yourself. This may seem irrelevant to you, perhaps even a little silly, but great power lies in the sound of your name, it is *your* vibration.

Hear your name announced as someone very special, very unique. For this is a true statement. Do not over-analyse everything … get out of your head … simply *feel* it, deeply, wholeheartedly.

Next, paste a photo of yourself here.

One that feels happy. Look at this picture of you with new eyes … with great appreciation, love, kindness, admiration and true acceptance.

FROM NOW ON you will start to see and think of yourself as a divine being, a spiritual being having a physical experience and not the other way round.

You are unified with *all* beings and *all* creation. You will begin to realise that all forms of separation are but an illusion in your mind, which keeps you in fear, in pain and in suffering. You are a divine being with infinite potential.

You may wonder how this thought will change your life? Perhaps you are thinking that these are intellectual theories, unobtainable in the world, not part of *your* reality. The key to this answer lies in the word *awareness*. Becoming aware of the self...deeply.

As your self-awareness increases, your inner and outer perceptions of everything will change and you will start to see beyond what meets the eye … you will start to see and *feel* the interconnectedness of all life. This is an AWAKENING. An awakening to your true Self.

In this book there will be different exercises, meditations and practical actions to do. They are meant to stimulate insights within, inspire new ways of being and to act as your reflection, your mirror. This will be a way for you to gain awareness of yourself as you are right now. You will need patience and tenacity to see things through. The more consistent your effort, the more effortless this journey will become. Herein lies the paradox. Remember that through discipline comes freedom.

Keep in mind that this book provides a safe non-judgmental space and opportunity for you to examine your thoughts, feelings and insights. My advice is to keep it private. This will also give you the freedom to truly speak your truth, as honesty is vital for real change to take place.

Please don't skip any exercises. Read this workbook from beginning to end. I suggest you stay with each chakra for at least a week, completing and integrating the exercises. Commit to these exercises fully. Really immerse yourself into doing them wholeheartedly. Once you have completed the book go back to any exercises you wish to review. Remember that each exercise will bring about some form of inner transformation. Do not underestimate the power of simplicity. Even if you feel that you do not really need to do an exercise, do it anyway. Each chakra exercise prepares for the following one, so it is important to cover all of the exercises.

What an exciting journey lies within!

Now, find a place that is quiet, somewhere you will not be disturbed. Read through this first and then once you are familiar with relaxing deeply, do the exercise. Close your eyes and take three long, deep breaths. One…two…three. Imagine yourself sinking down…down into the ground, down you go. You relax and you notice how all the tension just dissipates from your body. Take your time, there is no rush. Every muscle in your body relaxes completely. You start to count down from twenty. Nineteen … eighteen … seventeen … three … two … one … zero.

I want you to ask yourself this question: "What do I truly want?" Stay with this question for quite some time. See what arises.

Repeat this question a few times and notice if you answer differently. Remember what you answered and let the images, thoughts or feelings go.

Now I want you to see yourself. I want you to imagine yourself living the life you truly desire, being the person you wish to be - your best self.

Have you changed anything? If so, what? How are you different? What are you doing for a living? Have you dressed differently? Where are you living? What does your house look like? Are you travelling? Have you taken up a hobby you never dreamed possible? Have you made more friends? What is your passion? What drives, inspires and motivates you?

Perhaps you do not know; perhaps you are afraid of knowing, as this may take you out of your comfort zone. Perhaps you are lucky and know exactly what you want and what you would like to do, but feel trapped by the security of your present life. You may simply need to make a few minor adjustments.

Let us find out ... visualise as best you can, take as long as you need, give yourself permission to let your imagination take flight.

Do not worry if you leave something out. You can always come back to your visualisation at any time to make any changes to your mental image. Do not worry if you find it hard to visualise anything different, or if you just do not know what you would like to manifest.

This exercise is to start the process for you to tune into your creative potential of being able to create and re-create a reality of your choice. Whatever you focus on is what you will *attract* and *manifest*.

By imagining a life of abundance, happiness and success you are planting the seeds that in perfect time will germinate into your physical world. This energy already exists in thought form - it is simply waiting for you to command it into reality. Perhaps you have heard this all before? This is good. NOW is the time to start putting all your knowledge and wisdom into practice! You are an *infinite* being with infinite potential. Be as specific as you can in relation to the details of your vision, as this will help to speed up the manifesting process. Take your time.

Then slowly when you feel ready, start to count from one to ten. One ... two ... three ... eight ... nine ... ten. Slowly become aware of the room again. Feel your body and open your eyes. When you are finished, take time to write down all your thoughts and images concerning this exercise.

You may feel that you would like to repeat this exercise the following day, trust your intuition.

Nerise Howes

Notes on this exercise

FROM NOW ON, you will start each day with a short meditation. This is an integral part of this journey. By stilling your mind you are creating a space within to connect with your higher self, your divinity, as well as giving your busy mind a well deserved rest. This will greatly contribute to your ability to deal with stress more efficiently. It will help clarify your thoughts, slow down your ageing process, assist you in becoming more self aware and keep you focused on consciously raising your energy every day. Meditation and prayer go hand in hand. Prayer is talking to God while meditation is when you listen and experience God. Make space for both in your life. Each day, let your first and last thought be of God.

We will begin with a simple yet effective meditation. We will call it Finding the Space Within. Do not underestimate its power by its simplicity. Within this space is where the magic happens; this is where you make conscious contact with God.

God has many names. You may prefer to use other words such as Creator, Cosmic Energy, Light, Infinity or whatever resonates best with you. This is not a book on religion, it is about your connection to your self. It is coming from an understanding that you are essentially a spiritual being having an incredible physical experience here on earth.

Find a position that feels comfortable to you. You may choose to sit, kneel or lie down. Trust in what feels right. There is no right or wrong way to meditate. Set aside twenty minutes to half an hour for this practice.

Take three long, deep breaths, close your eyes, and let go of the outside world. All that you are going to do is to consciously follow your breath. As you breathe in, and out … your awareness will simply accompany your breath's journey. That is all.

At first it may seem like a struggle, as your mind will wander, it will chatter, it will do its utmost to distract you from this task. Be tenacious, patient and gentle with yourself. As time goes by you will notice a difference and what first started out as an inward struggle will gradually become more effortless in nature, something that you look forward to doing.

When your mind begins to wander and thoughts arise, simply observe them. Remain a witness. Remain objective and detached. Allow your thoughts to come and go, for as soon as you become attached to their development they will surely tempt you into seductive distraction. Observe your thoughts and come back to your breath. Follow the simple in and out rhythmic movement of the breath. Continue this process until your mind becomes less cluttered with fewer thoughts arising and you begin to feel in sync with your breathing rhythm.

Now you are ready for the next part of this meditation, which involves pausing between the two breaths. Breathe in, follow the movement of the breath, pause for three counts, holding the breath, breathe out, follow its movement, pause for three counts.

Continue this process. This *pause* is the *space* we are seeking. Within this space lies infinite potential, infinite creativity. As mentioned before, the space is where the magic happens, where you make conscious contact with God.

Step three involves accompanying your IN breath with the word *God* (or your substitute word), pause, now accompany your OUT breath with the word *love*, pause. *God* … (in) … *love* (out). Continue this process. This will add a powerful mantra (sacred sound) to your meditation.

Let's recap:
1. Following the breath with your awareness.
2. Doing the same process but now adding a pause or a gap between each breath.
3. Doing the same process, but adding the words *God* (or your substitute word) for the IN breath and *love* for the OUT breath with the pauses in between.

Do not analyse the whole process. Get out of your head and allow it just to happen. There are no words to effectively describe the outcome. It is in the experience itself and you need to remain patient and persevere. Set aside 20-30 minutes in the morning or evening each day.

If you are familiar with meditating and you find that another method works better for you, please feel free to use it instead of the above. I do encourage you to try this simple method for at least a week before you decide on using your own method. In the end, trust your intuition. Remember to start everyday with a meditation, you will feel the difference when you do not and it is an integral part of this process.

After you have completed the meditation repeat this phrase three times: I AM LOVE AND LIGHT DIVINE.

Now let us continue with our inner exploration. You are going to start working with each of the seven main chakras (energy centres relating to you physically, emotionally, mentally, and spiritually). We will explore and work with each one individually each week. From this you will be able to get a good picture of your energetic patterns.

I will not be going into great detail regarding each chakra as there are many good reference books available on this subject. But I will give enough information for you to do the practical exercises. At the back of the book I have included references on the psychology and nature of the chakras. For the purposes of the exercises a basic overall knowledge will be sufficient. You will be focusing on the application of the principles in your daily life through practical exercises. An in depth theoretical understanding is therefore not necessary.

The origins of the chakra system are found in the roots of the Hindu culture. The word "chakra" literally means wheel or disk in Sanskrit (an ancient Indian language). It dates back before 2,500 BC to the Vedas, which are the four Holy Books of the Hindus. But even before that, wise beings, mystics and yogis had passed down the knowledge of the seven "maps of consciousness".

The chakra system integrates many layers of the self- physically, emotionally, mentally and spiritually. In order for complete well-being, integrating as a ***whole*** being needs to be learned. You can think of the chakras operating a bit like valves that channel an electrical current throughout your body. They are interconnected, self-opening and subject to either functioning in excess or through deficiency, when out of balance. So the key is to ***balance*** these energies.

Any blockage or dysfunction in any one part of the chakra system affects all the other parts, therefore, it is vital to think of the chakra system as a whole integrated unit. When all the "wheels" are spinning in sync with each other and they are in harmony at the same speed, your energies will start to operate as a single unit. You will experience a state of good physical health, emotional equilibrium, mental awareness, clear thinking and spiritual unity.

Relax. You do not need to understand everything … simply trust and start the process of discovering your own chakra system.

BASE CHAKRA

This chakra relates to our physical needs and our survival in all its forms and variations.

Sanskrit name:	Muladhara
Translation:	Root or support
Location:	The base of the spine (between the genitals and anus)
Associated body parts:	The bones, skeletal structure, teeth, legs, feet and large intestine and governs the adrenal glands
Colour:	Red
Element:	Earth
Sound:	LAM or UH
Incense/oils:	Cedarwood, Patchouli, Musk and Lavender
Crystals:	Hermatite, Tiger's Eye and Blood Stone
Affirmation:	I have a right to be here.
	I nurture my body.
	I feel safe and secure in my life.

Remember to wear as much red as possible this week, to integrate this vibration.

FROM NOW ON I will love and honour my body. Everything that I choose to eat will nourish and nurture me. I will choose foods that give me the most nutrition, yet I will keep a sense of fun and balance, without obsessing over "good and bad" foods. Everything I put into my body will raise my energy levels. I will find a form of exercise to regularly put into practice. Write down how you can improve your choice of foods and what kind of exercise you will start. This needs to be integrated into your life *this* week.

Remember to stick with what you choose, be realistic, start off slowly, but make sure you keep at it! Maybe you could join a gym, start up some form of sport, start walking, swimming, yoga or take up dancing. Find out about Chakradance!

Plan for the week:

FROM NOW ON I will listen to my body's messages.

Remember that your body is a reflection of your thoughts. When your thoughts are out of alignment with your divinity or highest aspiration, you become dis-eased (diseased).

This exercise is two-fold:

Observing your thoughts and inner talk, then transforming them into positive healing ones, through affirmations.

Tune into your body. Write down what your body has to say to you. For example, "my back hurts". Explore this further. Why does it hurt? How did it start? What contributes to the pain? When does it feel better? What emotions arise when feeling the pain?

Examine these feelings. For example you may feel angry. Go deeper, search for the root cause. Notice the body part that corresponds to each chakra and explore the associated weak areas. For example, the base chakra governs the spine and skeletal structure. Make a note that your back hurts. This can relate to other issues regarding the base chakra energy in your life that may need shifting or balancing in some way. From this realisation perhaps you need to explore how supported you feel in your life.

This is a good place to look at your overall physical health. *Remember,* every illness holds a message for you. Listen. Listen. Listen. The more you can tune into your body's signals the better. Mentally scan through your whole body, noticing each part of your body.

Notes on this exercise

Connecting with Mother Earth is part of the healing process. This is very important to include in your programme while working with the base chakra.

Take a walk. Go somewhere quiet, somewhere peaceful, and somewhere beautiful. Find a place that makes your heart "sing". Climb a rock, take a hike, explore different parts of your country, and leave the city streets behind. Walk with bare feet on the grass, lie under the stars or go camping. Think of different ways to commune with nature. By connecting with nature there is a part of you that will connect with all creation and therefore with **yourself**. Spend as much time as you can just "being". Feel the earth beneath your feet, lie on the ground. Become aware of all the sights, sensations and sounds around you. Take notes of any images that come into your mind during these times. Write all your thoughts and feelings down. Even if they seem irrelevant, they never are.

Nerise Howes

Notes on this exercise

How does your prosperity picture look? Remember that you have created all of it … yes, including the lack of it.

You *can* re-create your wealth status by *changing your mental image* of what prosperity means to you, along with the set of belief systems you carry around with you. You can indeed affect the physical world by the way you use your mind. Prosperity is created and experienced in your mind. Creating money is applied in the same way as creating anything else in your life.

First of all you need to change your inner picture, which reflects any kind of lack in your life. This kind of scarcity consciousness, will keep you operating in this space unless you replace the mental image. Remember that you already *have everything* that you need to be prosperous.

You *are* already *whole*.

Really feel and absorb what I am saying.

When you operate from a point of "lack"- lack of money, talent, education, and experience - then you will simply be creating exactly that! You will find yourself constantly striving to have this special something that will make you whole, more complete, happy, successful or content. Everything you need is *already within*.

Begin to *believe* in your ability to effortlessly live the life you are meant to live, your divine reason for being here, your purpose. Abundance along with prosperity will follow naturally. Everything arrives in the perfect time to help you fulfil your dreams.

Believe that you *deserve* to live the life that you want. Cultivate a mental conviction that you are entitled to prosperity and abundance. Why shouldn't you be? There is enough to go around. Remember that prosperity in the form of wealth works the same way in that you will begin to see it coming into your life when you no longer need it or are attached to it. When you give of yourself and are in alignment with your purpose everything else will follow naturally. So most importantly, make this a journey of discovery. Find out what your purpose is, what do you have to offer to this world? Do not underestimate the difference your efforts can make. If you have no idea of what you feel you "should" be doing, ponder on this thought:

Living from a reference of *love* in every moment is already a purpose. Living this way, people will be able to feel the light radiating from within you. This energy will have a snowball effect on all those you come into contact with. Choose each moment wisely, with love and you *will* be living with intent and purpose. We will explore your life's purpose later on in this book.

Begin to act prosperous, right now. Living as a prosperous person is to be a generous person. Give freely to others and you will receive back. This is part of an invisible law of the universe. But do this without the expectation of receiving something in return, as the intention of giving is what is important here.

Please meditate on the word *abundance*. What does it mean and represent to you? Now let's take a look at your existing state of affairs.

Write down how much you currently earn.

Write down your weekly and monthly expenditures.

Write down your current debts.

Can you increase your income?

Are you wasting money? Can you be saving or using it more efficiently?

How can you become debt free?

Are you in a job that you enjoy? If not, what can you do to change it?

Remember that all things are possible. You need to know what you want first. Start with creating what it is that you want in thought form, visualise the image in your mind and then make an achievable plan to put into practice. Find a life coach if you need some professional help in making a financial plan. Perhaps you could brush up on some existing skills or make a fresh start by doing something that you love. The possibilities are endless. Do something that you feel passionate about.

Use this space to clarify your present financial situation. Answer the previous questions and make a plan to achieve your goals.

Nerise Howes

Notes on this exercise

Affirmation for prosperity:

"I am at peace each day, knowing that the source of my prosperity is God working through me and directing me."

Let's look at your connection with your "tribe" (your family and friends support network).

Describe your relationship with your father:

Describe your relationship with your mother:

Describe your relationship with your siblings:

Do you feel isolated? If you have answered yes, in what way?

Do you feel supported in your life?

Make a conscious decision to nurture your connection with your family and friends. Feeling part of a unit such as a family is important to feeling part of humanity and all of creation. A sense of "belonging" is healthy for the base chakra.

This week is about establishing a support network for you.

Things to do ...

Join a social group of like-minded people. Make some new friends. You may want to start a new hobby or join a discussion or meditation group. Trust your intuition. Rekindle existing friendships. Do things together.

Nurture family relationships. Make peace if need be and heal old wounds. Let go of past hurts, for these no longer serve you and will simply weigh you down. Clear the air; communicate with those close to you ... remembering that everyone is part of the same web of life, more closely connected than you can imagine.

FROM NOW ON start to truly *feel* a wonderful unity between everyone who crosses your path. Every person you meet or who plays a part in your life, plays a significant role in your awakening as a divine being!

Notes on this exercise

Does your home reflect who you truly are? How can you change it? How can you make it an outward expression of your inner self?

Firstly, your mission is to **get rid of clutter!** By letting go of the old you are making space for the new. Having clutter around creates stagnant energy. Detach yourself from that which you no longer need someone else can use it.

Focus on one room at a time. Create a beautiful space, somewhere you **want** to be.

Notes on this exercise

Nerise Howes

FROM NOW ON I will cultivate a non-violent approach in my life. I will respect all life remembering that everything created is sacred and that every living thing has a specific purpose in this life or it would not exist.

Being non-violent does not only apply on the physical level-as words and thoughts can be just as damaging to others and ourselves. It is therefore vital to constantly become aware of what we are thinking each and every moment.

In what ways can you become more non-violent? Think of every aspect of your life, physically, mentally and emotionally.

Notes on this exercise

I want you to meditate on, explore and think about the following words: What do they represent and mean to you?

Survival

Grounding

Roots

Earth

Physicality

Boundaries

Change

Security

Repeat three times out loud: I AM LOVE AND LIGHT
DIVINE

THE SACRAL CHAKRA

This chakra leads us from our basic existence to help us embrace what makes life worth living. It relates to our sense of pleasure, sexuality, nurturing, movement and change.

Sanskrit name:	Svadhistana
Translation:	Sweetness
Location:	The lower abdomen
Associated body parts:	Reproductive system (it governs the ovaries and testicles) and the urinary system (bladder, kidneys)
Colour:	Orange
Element:	Water
Sound:	VAM or Oo
Incense/oils:	Jasmine, Rose and Sandalwood
Crystals:	Citrine, Carnelion, Golden Topaz
Affirmation:	I am worthy of love and pleasure.

FROM NOW ON I let go of old, stagnant emotions that no longer serve me.

Focus on emotional release. Have an emotional clear out. Any event that still creates a strong emotion or sensation of any kind is unresolved and needs to be released or transformed. Emotions can become toxic if they are suppressed, they will drain your energy.

If you are not sure how you are feeling about something, simply tune in to your body. Your body is always in the present and will be your guide as to what is really taking place within your psyche or self. The more you can let go emotionally, the lighter and more alive you will start to feel energetically.

Remember that our bodies reflect our thoughts and emotions. Spend this week transforming anything that still creates negative feelings within.

Begin by vocalising your unexpressed feelings or write them down. You may feel you need to get professional help for example counselling, psychotherapy or body work such as deep tissue massage (your body will store all these energies). Trust your intuition. You may want to write a letter to someone (you don't have to send it). Find ways to express and let go of anger (punching cushions, working with sound and the breath, martial arts, dancing, sport). Spend quiet time meditating.

Firstly find a quiet space, somewhere you won't be disturbed. Mentally run through your life from being a child up until now. Write down any events or situations that bring up negative emotions. Make a conscious decision to neutralise these energies. Look beyond the external events and discover what is of real importance here. What could you have learned from the experience? Remember all events are ***neutral***. Once you are able to see the valuable lesson in each event you will be able to release it. It is as simple as that. Release the negative feeling and bless it with love.

Do not get caught up in blaming this or that person or circumstance. This is a trap that will keep you locked into playing the "victim" role when in fact you are completely in control in drawing each and every event to you, in order to gain deeper insight and understanding regarding yourself.

The golden rule is to accept ***full responsibility*** for everything that has happened in your life. Bless and thank each person who has played a role in this process, even if they brought up a lot of pain or anger. They have been a great teacher and mirror to you. Without this experience, inner growth could not have taken place. With this knowledge identify where you need to heal and grow and let go of stagnant emotions that no longer serve you. If you are unable to recognise the lesson or understanding gained from the experience, simply acknowledge the experience. This awareness will in time reveal the wisdom and insight you require. For now, just let it be. Bless it and move on to another experience.

Notes on this exercise

Water, water, water! Our bodies are made up of 70% water. You need to make sure you are drinking enough -between 8-10 glasses a day. Water is very beneficial for moving energy throughout your body. It is cleansing on many different levels. Go swimming this week. Take a trip to the beach, or sit by a lake or stream.

Meditate on the flowing movement or aspects of water and see how you can allow yourself to become more in touch with the natural flow of your life. I do not mean that you should allow yourself to get pushed and pulled by events or things of which you feel you have no control over...quite the contrary. **You** are the creator of your life! Move into new directions, find new ways of being and release any fears you may have of changing. Go with the flow of living fearlessly, remembering that you have infinite potential, you do not need to remain "stuck" in any areas of your life.

You are working with sexual energies in this chakra centre. You can also call it creative energies. It is simply the life force within. Through sex you are physically able to channel and express these energies. You are able to express your love to and for another being. It can be very beautiful and sacred. Unfortunately it is very easy to repress a lot of these energies because of fear and of course from social conditioning. What you need to do is to become aware of how you view and feel about your sexuality.

You will need openness, honesty and compassion for yourself. You will need the ability to take a step outside of your physical being to see the bigger picture of life. Finally you will need to see how to channel this great and powerful energy within, so that you may grow and expand as a spiritual being.

Write down all your feelings around your sexuality. Do you feel comfortable talking about sex? What beliefs do you hold regarding sex? What was your first introduction to discovering your sexuality? Have you been physically abused in the past? What are your physical boundaries like? Is there a recurring pattern regarding your sexual encounters and relationships with people?

Please seek professional help if you begin to feel overwhelmed by your emotions regarding these issues. There are many wonderful therapists who are trained to help you understand your feelings. Repressed emotions will find away to block your life energy, don't allow this to happen.

Notes on this exercise

In what way can you become more like water?

Where in your life do you feel stagnant?

Start to tune into your senses more. Everything can become a sensual experience. Start to see things with new eyes as if you are seeing something or someone for the very first time. Really begin to notice and pay attention to the beauty of each being or object. Become aware of the colours, shapes, smells and sensations.

This is the week for wearing as much orange as possible. Choose clothes that make you feel sensual. This chakra is governed by the more feminine, receptive kind of energy. If you happen to be a male in this life, remember that everyone contains both male and female energies within. Allow yourself to feel sensual, to feel alive, to feel attractive and desired.

Do not hold onto energies that are not serving you in a positive, uplifting way. Above all, let go of any judgement regarding yourself.

Nerise Howes

Notes on this exercise

What does sensuality mean to you?

FROM NOW ON I honour and celebrate my creative energies. I allow and welcome pleasure and creative expression into my life.

This is a very important exercise, although it may not seem so at first. You need to find a way to express your creativity. If you believe that you are not a creative type of person ... think again.

You are a multi-dimensional being with infinite potential. You are a co-creator in this world and the creator of your life! It is time to explore and develop this side of you.

This week you are going to do something creative. What have you always wanted to do but felt that you are not talented, skilled, young or old enough to do?

Join a group, class or simply start to explore the pursuit or hobby that you would like to do on your own. If you are unsure as to what you would like to do or try, simply pick anything and give it a go! You will soon see what it is that you do or don't enjoy...

Nerise Howes

Notes on this exercise

What do you feel passionate about?

How do you feel about your creativity?

Embrace change. For this next week you are going to change one small thing every day. Perhaps you could change the way you travel to work? By consciously changing something every day you are physically as well as mentally paving the way for bigger changes to take place within. Make this a playful exercise. Become more open and receptive to change in your life.

Notes on this exercise

What did you change? How did it feel?

FROM NOW ON I will be open to truly seeing my "shadow" sides. I will embrace all parts and aspects of myself without judgement, knowing that I have the power to change those parts that no longer serve me.

Firstly you need to become aware of the parts of yourself that you have repressed. Write down all the qualities and things that you dislike about yourself. Be truthful.

Once a shadow side has been seen, recognised and acknowledged, this energy is able to shift, balance and transform into something that serves you better. First you need to **understand** why it manifested within. Your shadow side carries a message and a jewel of wisdom. Make a list of the sides or qualities of yourself that bring you pain, embarrassment, isolation, confusion, anger, hurt, separation, disease, etc.

Nerise Howes

Notes on this exercise

Now I want you to look at this list with new eyes, with eyes that see the hidden strengths within each shadow quality, waiting to blossom into something beautiful.

I want you to make a list of all your beautiful qualities, talents and aspects. If you find yourself thinking something, but holding back on writing it down, as it seems too much like "blowing your own trumpet", then take your pen and write down, humility. Don't be shy. Don't hold back. Acknowledge that the positive within is something to be celebrated. This is your private space of sharing with and of yourself. You owe it to yourself to see things as they *are*.

Nerise Howes

Notes on this exercise

Now I want you to go back to the list you made of your "shadow" side qualities.

Next to each quality I want you to make notes of how you can transform each one into something that will serve you better.

Movements that will facilitate the shift and balancing of these sacral energies are Yoga, Thai Chi, Chi Gong and dancing, especially belly dancing and Chakradance.

Things you will need: a large piece of paper or cardboard, pencil, coloured pencils or paint and old magazines to cut out images and pictures.

What you are going to do is make a collage or picture of your life, as you would like it to be. Be as bold as you can. Create an image of all your dreams, visions and hopes.

Perhaps you are wanting to create a beautiful home, go travelling, pursue an interesting career, start a family... the more detail you can add the better.

You can cut out images that would represent all these wishes and desires. You may want to draw or paint, as you may find the images come to you in the form of an abstract kind of feeling. Whatever you choose to create will be what is needed for you at this present time to facilitate your personal and spiritual growth. Trust your intuition.

By creating these visual images you are starting to integrate this energy within and draw it down from the mental and spiritual plane into the physical realm of manifestation. This is a continuation of the very first visualisation you did regarding your life and how you would like it to be. We are now taking this exercise a step further by manifesting your thoughts into images and symbols you can physically see. Hang it up where you will notice it every day. Be wonderfully creative and have fun!

Nerise Howes

Notes on this exercise

FROM NOW ON I will follow the middle way. I shall remain balanced at all times. I will let go of extremism and become moderate in all things. While working with the second or sacral chakra, we need to look at how balanced we are in our lives. This chakra governs our feminine energy, the yin energy. We need to balance these energies with our masculine or yang energy.

A good place to start is by looking at your life and becoming aware of ways and areas where you are perhaps extreme in your behaviour or views.

Nerise Howes

Notes on this exercise

Are you addicted to anything?

In what ways can you bring more balance into your life?

Spend the following week practising moderation in all that you say or do. How does this feel?

I want you to meditate on explore and think about the following words. What do they represent and mean to you? What images, feelings and thoughts do they bring up physically, mentally, emotionally and spiritually?

Desire

Pleasure

Feminine

Nurturing

Movement

Commitment

Repeat three times out loud:

I AM LOVE AND LIGHT DIVINE

THE SOLAR PLEXUS

This chakra relates to self-transformation through developing a sense of power within.

Sanskrit name:	Manipura
Translation:	Lustrous gem
Location:	Between the navel and the base of the sternum. It governs the digestive system
Associated body parts:	Liver, stomach, small intestine and gall bladder
Colour:	Yellow
Element:	Fire
Sound:	RAM or OH
Incense/oils:	Ylang-ylang, Cinnamon, Bergamot
Crystals:	Yellow Citrine, Sunstone, Topaz
Affirmation:	I trust my inner source of power.
	I am my own person.
	I choose my thoughts and actions.

Remember to wear as much yellow as possible this week, to integrate this vibration.

FROM NOW ON I allow myself to shine. I allow myself to feel strong and powerful.

Please find and read Nelson Mandela's famous inaugural speech from 1994. It is written by Marianne Williamson "A return to Love: Reflections on the principles of a course in miracles". Simply type in key words from above on an Internet search engine such as Google and you are sure to find the reading.

I found the words of that speech to be very powerful as they truly touch each soul on a deep level. It is time to realise the immense power you have within. You are a spiritual warrior, a being made up of love and light, with infinite potential.

What would this mean to you, being a spiritual warrior?

What would it feel like to feel strong and self- reliant?

How would your life change, knowing that the power lies within, remembering that you are not separate from God and therefore divinely capable of all things?

With this knowledge you will start to feel more centred and more deeply connected to yourself.

We are going to play with this archetypal energy of the warrior. Close your eyes and imagine you are putting on a cloak. It is a beautiful cloak made out of exquisite fabric. See the colours; imagine what it would look and feel like. This is your spiritual warrior cloak. Put it on. Remember that once you are wearing this cloak you will notice an instant change. You will start to *feel* different. Notice your posture, your breathing and your movements. Do you feel you have a purpose? Do you feel more grounded? Do you feel fearless?

I want you to write down all your feelings and thoughts that come up once you put on your powerful cloak.

Notes on this exercise

For today you are going to rely completely on yourself. Your own inner guidance is sufficient. Ask help from no one. Trust your own feelings and intuition. Remember that you are totally responsible for drawing all situations and events to you. Each event is neutral. It is your reaction to the event that makes it either positive or negative, which in turn creates your pain, joy, suffering and bliss. So choose wisely, choose from *love*. Knowing this, your choices that you make will become in alignment with your higher self and you will gain the awareness that you truly do have the power within. You have all you need. You do not need to be wealthier, more successful, or talented to be a powerful force in this world. All that is required is to believe that you are not separate from God … not separate from all life.

So for today you will be once again wearing your spiritual warrior cloak. Be mindful that a true warrior has a strong sense of self and therefore does not feel the need to dominate others. A true warrior acts with humility, yet is assertive when he or she needs to be and speaks his or her truth authentically at all times, coming from a place of love.

Now, what would you like to accomplish with this lovely strong, dynamic, fearless and loving energy?

Notes on this exercise

On a physical level this chakra governs the digestive system. A good, physical clean-out of your body's system is always very beneficial for moving old stagnant energy. Liver cleansing is a good place to start, as the liver is very capable of storing emotions such as anger.

It is always wise to seek professional help and advice from a qualified healthcare worker.

When you repress a thought or feeling and do not allow it to be expressed in some way, you store that energy in your body and in your subconscious, where it will surface once again when triggered.

While you are working with cleansing the liver let us focus on anger.

Anger can be channelled once it has been recognised, owned and totally accepted. It is then possible to transform this energy into something constructive and positive. On the other hand, anger can become a destructive force if left to simmer, or if ignored or denied. You may experience physical symptoms as your body tries to give you the message that something is out of balance within. You may experience disease. You may show signs of depression or suffer from stress and insomnia.

You may also feel as if you are riding an emotional roller coaster, constantly reacting or over-reacting to situations, or you may simply feel out of sorts and frustrated without knowing why. Does any of this sound familiar?

Here are some ideas of how to let go of anger in the body. If you are afraid of what might come up for you during this exercise, remember there are many wonderful compassionate people who dedicate their lives to helping others deal with strong emotions. Do some research into finding the right therapist for you.

I do believe that you would be able to do a lot of the releasing work yourself if you don't have a history of severe emotional stress. Punching cushions in the privacy of your own home can seem a silly thing to do, but it helps to release emotional energy in a physical way. Combine this process with verbalising your feelings.

Talk to an imaginary person. Express your thoughts and feelings clearly and truthfully. The moment an emotion is voiced, it loses its power. This is a perfect time to communicate any unresolved issues with other people. Lack of communication can so easily distort what is truly taking place between two people. But if this is not an option, then simply have the intention of your words reaching the person without them being physically present. Hearing yourself speak your feelings out loud brings clarity to your thoughts and the situation.

A very good way to let go of old anger and stuck energy is to write down all your feelings and thoughts. If you have already done this exercise previously, repeat it and see if anything different comes up for you this time.

Allow yourself to say everything you need to say, remembering that it is a private exercise and that you can throw it away afterwards. Write a letter to the person you need to communicate with or write a letter to yourself ... don't hold back. Say it all and then let it go. Once you have acknowledged these feelings, they will be much easier to detach yourself from, as the power that they once held has now been released. These feelings are no longer held in the dark or in the shadow. They have lost their power over you.

It is always a good idea to work on the physical level while shifting energy, so do something physical. Go for a run; notice how different you feel afterwards. Make some form of exercise part of your daily or weekly routine.

Receive a form of bodywork such as deep tissue massage to loosen up tense muscles that are holding stored past emotions. Move, move and move some more. This will help with the flow of energy within. It has been scientifically proven that people who do less exercise have higher levels of stress.

Nerise Howes

Notes on this exercise

How do you express or repress your anger?

FROM NOW ON I will cultivate being positive and optimistic in all things. I will start to live from a place of joy and cheerfulness.

Why is this important? Everything is a vibration. The higher something vibrates the more joy, happiness and positivity will be present. Vibrations that are similar in nature will attract each other. So if you want to attract joy and happiness, be happy, be joyful. The more optimistic you are able to be in any given circumstance, the more you will be able to contribute to raising the energy around you, which in turn will benefit all of humanity.

Nerise Howes

Notes on this exercise

FROM NOW ON I take full responsibility for my emotions.

Blaming others for the way we feel, comes from not being able to see the bigger picture of why our relationships with others are so important to our personal growth.

You consciously and unconsciously draw each and every situation and person to you. Every person and event is simply a mirror for us, a teacher. Every human emotion lies dormant within each of us waiting to be triggered by an event, something someone says or does or from any external experience. This creates the drama of our lives. It is very easy to become caught up in this process of constantly reacting to external stimuli. It is very easy to take things personally and then to blame others for the way we feel. But by consciously taking responsibility for our emotions, we are then able to see where healing is needed. We can then let go of out-dated thoughts and beliefs that no longer serve us. All events are ***neutral***. Our reactions are not and this is where the pain and suffering comes into play. The good part is that we have the power to ***choose*** again. So, decide to choose a different response that will bring you joy and happiness from now on …

Taking full responsibility for all your feelings and thoughts will bring much freedom as you will no longer see yourself as a victim.

Nerise Howes

Notes on this exercise

Mostly fear arises from the "unknown". When there is an understanding regarding something, fear dissolves. Fear arises when you *separate* yourself from the great life force. When you feel that your survival is threatened in some form, you contract into fear. This stems from a lack of understanding when you solely identify with your body, whereas in affect you are so much more. You are an eternal being simply choosing to have an earthly experience in a physical vehicle (body). Trust and surrender… two powerful words.

Notes on this exercise

What are you afraid of? List all of your fears.

Where in your life can you surrender and trust more?

I want you to explore each fear. Become familiar with what arises in your mind and body, as you imagine and visualise the fear. What physical or emotional sensations do you experience?

Now let go of the fear and clear your mind. Come back to the same fear later but this time look with new eyes and a new understanding.

All beings are linked together, forever. So if you fear the loss of someone or something, remember this: there is *no* separation. Death is simply a moving from one place to another, as if you are going on a trip. You do not cease to exist, quite the opposite. You simply put on a "new set of clothes". Your soul is *eternal*. With this thought firmly in your mind ... what else is there to fear?

All fears can be dissolved. Start to view them as little "helpers" that show you where you need to focus your attention on, in terms of healing something within or simply realigning yourself with the greater truth.

Next to each fear that you have listed, I want you to write a way in which you can transform each one. In what way can you actively participate to overcome these fears?

For example you may fear speaking in public. What can be done about this? Firstly, look at what lies behind the fear. What could be the worst that would happen? People may laugh at you. People may ignore you. People may reject you, dislike or disagree with you. You may feel physically ill, forget what you had to say, stutter, not be able to project your voice, et cetera.. Now *feel* these things. In your mind play through each scenario. *Feel* the fear within. *Choose* again. Choose a different reaction to this event, one that will create all the opposite outcomes. Play this out in your mind. Visualise the details. Feel how wonderfully *effortless* it is to simply share something with others. Speak from your heart. Be authentic. Be natural. Relax into the process. Everyone has the potential to experience each fear and joy, just like you. So choose to speak from a place of *love* and there will be no space for fear. All of the things that you try to avoid feeling, such as rejection and being laughed at, are *your illusions* that you have created again and again. Other people's opinions ***do not change who you are*** … and who you are is much greater than your present personality. Feel this deeply. Understand the energy behind these words.

Notes on this exercise

Do you have any regrets? Perhaps you feel you could have gone to university, followed a different life path or career, taken a special holiday, paid more attention to your children, not have made a hurtful remark to someone you love etc. It is important to become aware of these feelings as once they are acknowledged you will be able to move on by transforming these energies into positive reminders of where healing is called for. Emotions such as feeling regret can be very draining energetically.

Write down any regrets you may have. Remember this is about becoming aware of these feelings. It is not about dwelling on how things could have been if you had done this or that ...

Notes on this exercise

FROM NOW ON I believe I am fully capable of manifesting my goals, visions and dreams.

Firstly, you need to be able to see what it is that you desire. *Visualisation*. This is a very powerful exercise. Remember that *you create* your world. The energy that you send out will come back to you, so choose wisely. Try to include as much detail as possible. Remember it is never too late to create the life that you desire.

Start by seeing an overall vision. Then begin to break this life vision down into steps of how you can achieve and manifest your dreams and goals. These must be practical steps that you can easily put into action. All that is left for you to do is to surrender and know within that your life purpose will unfold as it is meant to be.

If you find it difficult to visualise anything different than what you experience in your life at present, yet you feel discontent or restless, ask and you *shall* receive.

Simply say this: "I am ready to fulfil my life's purpose. I surrender to Thy will, the will of infinite knowledge and understanding. I am ready to awaken and to become a channel for love and light."

This is all that is required. Be open to little messages, coincidences or images that may come to you during the day or within your dreams at night. There are no wrong turns that you can take in your path; each is a way that perfectly facilitates your personal and spiritual growth. So be at peace, knowing this.

Write down your dreams and goals, including the steps you need to take in order to achieve them. Begin with the overall vision and then break it down into blocks of five years, then each year, each month and finally each week. Trust whatever feels right in terms of how far ahead you project. There are no rules to this exercise. If you are only able to see long- or short-term goals, don't worry, that is fine. Your goal plan is totally unique, so allow it to manifest as it comes to you.

Notes on this exercise

FROM NOW ON I consciously choose not to give my personal power away to anyone or anything. Without your personal power you will be a victim in your life. Whenever you start to feel drained or overwhelmed by any external situation or experience, remember that you are energetically plugged into the infinite power of God. Tune into receiving this energy to keep up your levels of personal power. You may want to use the symbolic exercise of putting on your warrior cloak during times when you need to feel stronger within. While using your personal power wisely, find ways to use it to be of service to God and humanity.

Notes on this exercise

In what way can you be of service to God and others?

In what way do you give your personal power away? How can you change this?

I want you to meditate on, explore and think about the following words. What do they represent to you? How do they make you feel physically, mentally, emotionally and spiritually?

Action

Confidence

Individuality

Power

Purpose

Transformation

Masculine

Repeat three times out loud:
I AM LOVE AND LIGHT DIVINE

THE HEART CHAKRA

This chakra relates to developing true self-acceptance, forgiveness, compassion and unconditional love.

Sanskrit name: Anahata
Translation: Unhurt
Location: Centre of the chest
Associated body parts: The thymus gland, the heart, lungs, arms and hands
Colour: Emerald green
Element: Air
Sound: YAM or AH
Incense/oils: Melissa, Rose
Crystals: Jade, Emerald, Malachite, Green Calcite
Affirmation: I love and accept myself completely.
                         I extend love in all that I say and do.
                         I extend love in all that I say and do.

Remember to wear as much green as possible this week, to integrate this vibration.

This is a very powerful exercise and goes hand in hand with one of the affirmations for this week. Sit in front of a mirror. Now, take a few nice, long, deep breaths. Feel centred and calm. Gaze into your eyes. If it feels strange, allow it to be so. Keep eye contact with yourself. After a while, say your affirmation out loud: "I love and accept myself completely". Play around with emphasising each word in turn, so that you would say: I *love* and accept myself completely. Remain with this phrasing then change to: *I* love and *accept* myself completely, then: I love and accept *myself* completely, et cetera.

Notice what arises within. Does it make you laugh, cry or feel silly? Write everything down (after the exercise, not during the process). Repeat this exercise many times, as much as possible. Keep with it. Really *feel* the words. Really *see* yourself with new eyes … with loving eyes … start to feel deep compassion for yourself.

Notes on this exercise

Unconditional love. What does this mean to you?

FROM NOW ON I will see every being and creature as a face of God.

Visualise yourself connected to everyone you meet through an invisible cord. Start to consciously look past a person's behaviour and see the divinity within them. Send a loving thought to every person you meet in the day. Wish them silently a blessing of happiness, healing or whatever arises in your mind that will increase their energy level, simply by your intention.

This is a wonderful exercise. Notice how you feel. What inner thoughts and feelings does this exercise bring up for you?

Notes on this exercise

Forgiveness. This is a ***very*** powerful word. Its value to completely transform your being and life is underestimated to say the least. It is time to ***release*** all those old worn out energies that keep you locked in your guilt.

Firstly, you need to forgive ***yourself***. This can be quite an emotional experience as you bring up past hurts that you no longer need to carry around. Make a conscious decision right here, right now, to let go of all your guilt and forgive yourself for whatever you feel you did or didn't do in the past. In the bigger scheme of things none of the past matters anymore. You gained an insight by choosing in a certain way and now you know better. You have more understanding and you are able to make a different choice, one that creates joy, harmony and love. Be thankful for the experience or you would not have gained the insight. Write down everything you feel you need to forgive yourself for ... any guilt.

Write it all down so that you can empty your mind and see in black and white what it is that is keeping your heart from being "unhurt" (the meaning of this chakra). You may have done the similar exercise during the sacral chakra, but do it again here as you work with the heart chakra. If you have already released the emotion of a certain experience, you will feel neutral when thinking about it. If you do not, continue the process.

Go back to when you were a child and continue reviewing your life up to the present. Remember that any event that still brings up any kind of negative emotion is unresolved. By doing this exercise you are creating a space for something new to take its place. Mentally see how the event changes as you consciously forgive and bless everyone involved with love and understanding.

Now take a look at the forgiveness list once again, this time with compassion and love. Know that you did the best you could from the knowledge and the understanding that you had at that point in time. All experience is of value. Nothing can change the fact that you are a beautiful, divine being. Your choices may not always be in alignment with the truth but herein lies the blessing: you have the power to choose again, differently.

Repeat out loudly: "I forgive myself for all that I have done in the past ... things which may have created pain, fear or hurt ... I forgive myself and I let it go."

You now have a blank page to create whatever you want. Simply decide to choose from *love* and you cannot go wrong. What would you like to create now?

Nerise Howes

Notes on this exercise

Life consists of a continual interplay between two forces; giving and receiving. Think of your breathing. You cannot hold your breath for too long before you become very much aware that you need to exhale and take in another breath. This is the natural flow of all life. This balance between letting go (giving) and receiving is part of everything that you do. You need to be open to receive, so you need to allow yourself the space for new thoughts, new experiences and new ways of being. You also need to be able to receive love from those around you, but you can only recognise this love when you are open to it. Surrender all fear from being hurt.

Give of yourself. What I mean by this is to extend love to all those who come into your life without judgement. The process of loving is as natural as exhaling. You have come here to learn how to extend love. This should become your uppermost thought. When you seek love, you will struggle, as the love you so desperately seek is *already within*. All you need to do is to allow it to be expressed in some form and way every day, each moment. You cannot find love outside of yourself; you cannot find that which is already there. People and events in your life are not the source of your love or the reason you "lack" it. In other words your love is *not* depended on anything external to you. You simply need to acknowledge and become aware of the love already within.

Notes on this exercise

In what way can you become more receptive to receiving love?

In what way can you add a little more light to the world and those you meet along the way?

How can you extend your love more effectively? Think of practical ways. Think of everyday opportunities. Remember you do not need to go to far away places to offer your love (you can if you want to).

Every time you meet someone or find yourself in any kind of situation, it is a golden opportunity for you to put into practice your most natural talent; to love.

FROM NOW ON I choose to develop a sense of playfulness. I allow myself to be "silly" and childlike. I connect with my innocence within.

Today is the day for having fun! You are going to be playful and free, free from any thoughts of "what will people think", being ridiculed, being laughed at, free from thinking you are too old, too overweight, too wise, too intellectual, too lady like, too masculine or too educated.

It may seem a little strange and unfamiliar at first, especially if you are not used to expressing yourself in a creative way ... but stick with it! Remember that you are a multi-dimensional being with many sides; so don't limit yourself to the character you have created for yourself this far.

Allow yourself to be open and receptive to doing things in a different way. Have more fun and be playful. Laugh more. See the funny side to things and interact.

You may want to choose one time in the course of the day to have fun or you may choose to let this playful energy flow into your whole day or week. Perhaps you may even cultivate the possibility of including this playfulness into your life on a continual basis.

Explore and experiment. Remember to come from a space of innocence and love; making fun of other people in a hurtful way will only create negative energy. You may choose to do this exercise by yourself at first. This is quite fine. Sing along in the car on the way to work. Be spontaneous, allow yourself to simply **Be. Have fun!**

Nerise Howes

Notes on this exercise

FROM NOW ON I will not take things personally.

Remember this bit of wisdom. Nothing other people do is **because of you**. It is because of them. Everybody lives in his or her own mind or dream, which is different to the world that you perceive. By taking something personally you make an assumption that the other person knows **your** world, the world **you** have created from all of **your** experiences. Others are coming from a different place, created by the sum total of **their** experiences. Things will therefore always look different.

Other people do not have the power to "hurt" you by what they say. What is hurting you is simply an open wound that becomes sensitive by what has been said, this triggers the pain. The process stems from old belief systems and programming that has not been released or healed within. The other person acts as your "mirror" to show and remind you of what needs to be changed, healed and ultimately transformed.

What you most dislike about someone is what you most **deny within yourself**.

Start to see other people in a different way ... their presence in your life is a blessing; they are helping you grow, as you help them in return. Nothing they say or do is a personal attack on you; it is simply their reaction to certain stimuli, based on their previous experiences.

Before you **react** to something someone says, pause for a moment. Consciously choose a different response. See the bigger picture here and **choose** to respond from a different space, other than one from hurt, frustration, anger or past fears. Your reaction to a previous hurt makes you react in a similar way in the present. Your motivation should not be to try to prevent yourself from getting hurt by avoiding life - avoiding intimacy and closeness - but by cultivating a strong sense of self within. This comes from your awareness and understanding that **your are love**. This will give you security in your own being and fear in all its disguises will automatically fall away. Remember that everyone acts from his or her level of understanding and therefore consciousness.

Nerise Howes

Notes on this exercise

FROM NOW ON I will let go of all judgement. When you judge someone, you are creating separation. This process always leads to fear and ultimately to some kind of pain or suffering. Fear can manifest in many different ways through anger, jealousy, resentment, frustration and criticism to name a few.

As soon as someone or something is labelled, the real essence of the person or experience is lost. Through the way that you perceive yourself, the other person or the situation, the once expansive quality of the person or object now no longer exists. Someone or something has been judged, contained and therefore limited. They ceased to exist as unlimited potential the moment the judgement was made. For example saying that this is a flower, more specifically a rose, defines this once mysterious creation into something that now has a name, certain qualities and a specific purpose. In this physical world we name things or objects in order to communicate about them. Through this process we create separation between one object and another. This is necessary for the experience of living in this physical plane of duality and opposites. In time our level of understanding will expand and allow for us to see beyond these physical boundaries realising that all creation is in fact unified as one form of energy. We simply interpret everything we see as separate entities or objects.

When we judge others or ourselves we limit this infinite potential. This inhibits the process of change and growth. So consciously decide right here, right now to refrain from criticising or judging. Allow things to simply be. It is not your job to try to change people or to "save" the world. Negative criticism only succeeds in creating more negative energy. For where we focus our attention, is where and how the energy will manifest in the physical realm, as like attracts like.

Spend today becoming aware of when and how you judge. Remain in the present. Let go of your need for approval from external sources. Herein lies great freedom. Choose to respond to others from a space of love. Note how this changes the energy between you and the other person.

Nerise Howes

Notes on this exercise

FROM NOW ON I will cultivate a sense of ***gratitude***.

It is very easy to forget how many blessings we have … how many wonderful, beautiful beings and things are present in our lives. Let us count these blessings.

Write down all the things in your life that make your heart "sing". Think of friends, family, your health, your home, experiences you've had, places you have visited. Think of everything that touches you in a special way. Is there anything you take for granted in your life?

Nerise Howes

Notes on this exercise

Take a trip down to the beach, a forest, a park or anywhere special. You are going to find yourself a beautiful stone, a shell or any object that catches your eye. This is going to become your **gratitude** object. It will help remind you of all the wonderful blessings you have in this life.

Keep this object next to your bed. Each morning and night pick it up, while holding it start to feel a deep inner gratitude for all that you have in this life. Give thanks for all the blessings of friendship you share, the food that you eat, the home that you live in and for everything good in your life. This object will represent anything that deserves your gratitude. This includes even the painful experiences that have given you insight and understanding along the way.

This is a very powerful soul action. Don't underestimate the power and importance of this process. From this space you will begin to experience a sense of belonging here in this world. You will awaken to being present in each moment, for each is sacred. There are no ordinary moments, only opportunities to grow. For this gift, give thanks everyday.

Nerise Howes

Notes on this exercise

FROM NOW ON I will cultivate compassion. Remember that when another person suffers in any way, in truth you are suffering too. The Eternal Self or God-Mind lives within all people. We are all part of this energy. In what way can you become more compassionate?

How can you practically demonstrate compassion in the world? Perhaps you could become involved with an association for a good cause or support a charity you feel needs it. Perhaps you could visit the lonely, the elderly or the sick. There are many ways that you could become involved in your community by extending love and compassion to those in need. But also remember that charity indeed does begin in the home. How can you become more compassionate towards your family and those closest to you?

Nerise Howes

Notes on this exercise

Practice deep breathing every day. Breathe from your diaphragm. The element associated with the heart chakra is air, so you need to consciously become aware of how you are breathing. Notice the times that you hold onto your breath. Your breaths connect you to all of life and of course to *yourself*, so *breathe!*

I want you to meditate on, explore and think about the following words. What do they represent to you? How do they make you feel physically, mentally, emotionally and spiritually?

Balance

Freedom

Love

Relationship

Peace

Acceptance

Expansion

Repeat three times out loud:

I AM LOVE AND LIGHT DIVINE

THE THROAT CHAKRA

This chakra relates to how we express ourselves.

Sanskrit name:	Vissudha
Translation:	Purification
Location:	Throat centre
Associated body parts:	Thyroid, parathyroid, ears, neck, throat and shoulders
Colour:	Blue
Element:	Ether
Sound:	HAM or EYE
Incense/oils:	Chamomile, Myrrh
Crystals:	Turquoise, Aquamarine and Lapis Lazuli
Affirmation:	I always speak my truth.
	What I have to say is worthy of being listened to.

Remember to wear as much blue as possible this week, to integrate this vibration.

FROM NOW ON I will speak my truth. Your voice reflects a lot about you. It reveals the state of your physical, mental and emotional health. Your voice is *your* sound, your vibration. It is a reflection of how you have been focusing your attention and awareness in the past up to the present.

From this process a certain kind of energy has been created that is revealed by the sound of your voice. You can say that your character shapes your voice. Your voice may change according to the kind of energetic patterns you choose to create. These energies are then manifested into a certain specific physical sound. Your body is a vehicle to communicate through, with and from. And yes, the shape of your body, the length and thickness of your vocal chords and the shape of your mouth are all factors that play a definite role in determining the type of sound that will emanate from your body. But the voice conveys a lot more. The famous Greek philosopher Socrates wrote: "Speak, that I may see you".

Firstly, let's explore your voice. What does an *authentic voice* mean to you? How do you feel about your voice? Describe your voice. Be as objective as you can. Do you hold back from saying things? When? In what kind of situations do you feel less able to open up? Perhaps you experience the opposite and find yourself unable to stop talking in social settings, to the extent that people try to avoid a conversation with you? What do you think other people hear when they listen to your voice?

Notes on this exercise

An authentic voice speaks from the **heart**. An authentic voice communicates clearly. It is a voice that exudes passion, honesty, compassion and trust.

If you want to work on your voice, work on yourself. There are many different vocal exercises that help to clear stagnant energy stored within the body. Toning, chanting and sound release techniques are good ways to unblock this throat chakra energy. Find information on how to tone and chant. There are many good books written on this subject. Working with the different sounds from each chakra (chanting the sound regularly) will also help to shift energy.

It is important to keep breathing deeply from your diaphragm as this facilitates the production of a strong yet relaxed voice.

Record your voice. Speak into a microphone and play the recording back. Listen to your present everyday voice with an objective ear. Do this before you start to work on your voice. After a week of vocal toning, re-record your voice and notice any changes, feelings and insights from this exercise.

Notes on this exercise

What can you release vocally? What has not been expressed in the past and present? This is the time to **communicate**. Make a point of contacting anyone you need to "clear the air" with. It is very easy for thoughts and feelings to become distorted when something is left unspoken. This is where *forgiveness* comes into play. Be open and receptive to hearing what the other person has to say, while remaining centred. Remember to pause before reacting from a space of hurt. Responding from a place of love and understanding, yet speaking your truth, will help to dissolve any negative feelings. You will feel as if something has been lifted from your shoulders after doing this exercise. There is no point carrying "excess baggage" around with you any longer. Let go and resolve any issues or misunderstandings with everyone who has come into your path. Now.

Notes on this exercise

Having a balanced throat chakra also relates to how you *listen*.
FROM NOW ON I will truly listen.

Start to listen from your whole being. Words are sacred, but there is more to listen to, other than just words. It is the energy behind the words that you need to tune into, as well as all the other subtleties that present themselves to you in so many different ways.

When you are listening to someone, really focus your energy on them. This way you will both be tuning into a similar frequency and the communication will flow more easily. Spend today *really* listening ... listening to others in a more focused way and tuning into yourself. Notice what goes through your mind during the course of the day. Listen to your inner talk. Is it positive or negative? Does it heal or harm your sense of self worth?

I want you to monitor your thoughts. Each time you have a negative thought write it down. At the end of the day, count them.

Do not underestimate the power of your thoughts. They are the building blocks for your physical manifestations. You have heard many times that what you think is what you will attract to you. This is true, it is a natural law of the universe. Everything is a vibration. You need to cultivate an environment that grows beautiful seed thoughts, which in turn will flower into beautiful manifestations.

Start to eradicate all harmful inner talk by replacing each one with a positive uplifting thought. This requires commitment and a desire to choose from a space of wholeness and love. Using affirmations can be a powerful way to transform negative inner talk and create a new space for being.

Begin to listen and trust your intuition. Ask to receive an answer to any question you may have, then be patient and open to receiving these messages in some form. The answers may not always come in the way that you would expect. Always remember that your soul knows exactly what it needs in order to awaken and grow.

Notes on this exercise

You are going to start tuning into your energy field. Your physical body is not the only "body" that you have. You also have more subtle bodies on an emotional, mental and spiritual level. Each one vibrates at a specific frequency, equal to the light quota that your being radiates. The etheric body or light-body forms a vehicle for your soul to move around in, which is independent from your physical body. Think of yourself similar to an onion, consisting of many different layers. The layer closest to your body is the physical layer which reveals your state of health - how at ease or dis-eased your physical body is.

A little further away from the physical body you will find the emotional aura, representing emotional balance. Then further out from this layer you find the mental layer, revealing your intellectual and mental activity. Finally you come to the outer spiritual layer, which is linked to more subtle higher levels of being.

It is important to protect these subtle energies, just as you create boundaries for your physical self. There are many ways to do this.

A simple yet effective way is to simply surround your whole self with light. You can do this mentally, through visualisation. Enclose yourself entirely with a bubble of beautiful white or golden light. Do this whenever you feel as if your energy is being drained, when you are in a place where there are many people, whenever you feel low, tired, uneasy or run down.

Let us take this a step further ...

In your mind's eye I want you to imagine yourself made up entirely of light ... your physical body dissolves and all you can see and feel are the vibrating particles of light. Gradually you begin to increase the intensity of this light, so that you transform into a beautiful, shimmering radiance that vibrates with a clear, strong and loving energy. Embrace this feeling and visualisation.

FROM NOW ON begin to see and feel yourself as a being made of light. Spend each day for the rest of the week with this image and visualisation. The more you can focus on the light within, the more you will naturally begin to emanate this higher kind of frequency.

Notes on this exercise

A powerful exercise to include into your daily routine and practice is the use of saying, thinking or chanting the names of God. This keeps you focused on staying in a raised level of energy. Notice the shift of your energy when you are angry, upset or afraid and you start chanting the name of God. You will feel as if you are pulled right out of that lower frequency. It brings you from your lower self to your higher self, very quickly. What I mean by lower and higher selves is simply the space where your attention has been focused, either from a place of love or a place of fear or separation. This is a separation from your true self, which is divinely connected to all life and united with God. Experiment in using different names for God and then choose one that you prefer for the duration of this exercise.

Mantras are sacred sounds, for example you may be familiar with AUM. Many of these sacred sound combinations actually do exist in the higher realms or dimensions of being. The ancient Indian seers or "Rishis" were able to tune into these powerful sounds, by hearing them clairaudiently and then bringing them into the human realm.

The power of these mantras is truly great. The more a mantra is used, the more powerful it becomes. The use of sound can heal, but it can also destroy. Your words can be an inspiration or they may create a negative energy. Herein lies great power, for you, to consciously choose your words with care and wisdom.

The names of God, or mantras, help to align individual consciousness with the God consciousness. They help us remember our true nature, our true divinity, as the eternal self. Using these mantras is a great way to consciously raise your energy and vibration at all times.

Here are a few names you may wish to use:

I am that I am
AUM
OM
Brahma

Vishnu
Shiva
God
Shalom
Elohim
Hare Krishna
Om Shanti
Allaha Akbar
Ave Maria
Christ
Great spirit of Light
Love

If none of these resonate with you, find your own. Remember it is the *intention* behind the words and the energy of the sound, which creates the power. Any name or quality of God will create your desired result. Trust your intuition. Write down your words or names of power here:

You may find it useful to begin the day with your meditation followed by the chanting of your mantra and the saying of your affirmations. You may simply want to find words of power to use throughout your day as you desire or when the occasion arises. My advice is to make your words of power or mantra part of your inner vocabulary.

Nerise Howes

Notes on this exercise

I want you to meditate on, explore and think about the following words. What do they represent to you? What feelings, thoughts and sensations do they bring up physically, emotionally, mentally and spiritually?

Self-expression

Truth

Shyness

Communication

Individuality

Repeat three times out loud:

I AM LOVE AND LIGHT DIVINE

THE THIRD EYE CHAKRA

This chakra relates to our intuition and perception.

Sanskrit name:	Ajna
Translation:	Perceive and command
Location:	Between the eyebrows
Associated body parts:	The pineal gland and the eyes
Colour:	Indigo, which is similar to the colour of the night sky
Element:	Light
Sound:	SHAM or AYE
Incense/oils:	Hyacinth, Rose, Geranium
Crystals:	Amethyst, Azurite, Purple Apatite
Affirmation:	I trust my intuition.

Remember to wear as much indigo as possible this week, to integrate this vibration.

FROM NOW ON I choose to see the beauty in all things. Simply by making this conscious decision, your perceptions will begin to change. Spend today really *seeing*. Notice details, colours, shapes and patterns. When you look at something, imagine it is the very first time that you are seeing it. Cultivate a sense of childlike wonder and awe for the complexity of its creation. Become aware of what catches your eye … it could be anything!

Notice how focusing on the beauty of an object or person changes an inner feeling of connection with them. Start to look beyond your physical eyes, using your inner eye. See, feel and sense everything you see as a vibration. On a deeper level become aware that all creation and all beings are linked and connected. Tune in to all of your senses and notice how everything that you see begins to look different. Your inner perceptions are changing. You are beginning to SEE the bigger picture: everything is a reflection of self. You are not separate from anyone or any part of creation. ***Expand*** this ***awareness***.

Write down any thoughts, feelings or sensations that came up for you, after focusing on ***really seeing*** today …

Notes on this exercise

Spend time in silence. This is a very important exercise to do in order to tune into your inner self and to start using your intuition more effectively. Firstly, find silence in your day. This can be your meditation time in the morning or evening. While working with this chakra, it may be beneficial to add on a little extra time (simply an extra 15 minutes) to your meditation session.

Taking it a step further, make an effort to find a whole day where you can go somewhere quiet, somewhere in nature. Try not to communicate with anyone. If you have family commitments, you may have to plan this exercise ahead. Find a friend or family member that will be willing to look after any children or pets for that day. Pack a lunch and take it with you so that you don't have to engage in any kind of communication while purchasing your food. Don't take a book to read, music to listen to or any other activity. This day is about ***not doing*** and simply ***being***. Take a pen and notebook, in case you want to jot down any thoughts.

Make use of the silence and peacefulness of the place you have chosen for this exercise. During this quiet time, clear your mind. Don't allow yourself to worry about anything or anyone for the duration of this exercise. Your life will be waiting for you when you get back. This is a time to tune into yourself, without being distracted or turning your attention away to someone else or some other activity. There is nowhere you need to go and nothing to do. It is simply a time for you to be by yourself and to feel at peace.

Notes on this exercise

FROM NOW ON I will tune into the synchronicities in my life.

All you have to do is become aware of any "coincidences" that happen. The smallest, most seemingly insignificant occurrence can have a tremendous impact on your life! Pay attention. Remember that everyone is linked and connected. Each person you meet is a teacher and a messenger. We are all helping each other grow and expand our consciousness.

For today, tune into this way of thinking … ask a question in the morning (any question) and see what unfolds during the next few days. For example, you may just happen to catch a glimpse of an article on a notice board or in the paper that reminds you of something, which leads you to contact a certain person who indirectly gives you a solution or answer to your question. See what I mean? There are many ways in which you may receive messages relating to your questions.

Begin to see your life as an adventure unfolding each day, each moment. Pay attention to the signs and directions given to you for this life's journey. The more you tune into this way of viewing your life's events and experiences, the more these synchronicities will arise to help shape your life and the more connected you will begin to feel connected to your purpose.

Everything you have experienced up until now has been the best possible way for you to *awaken*! Every event has brought you *here*. This present moment offers you the message that you have been seeking all long. It is time! Arise from your slumber and your illusion of who you are, why you are here and where you are going...You are an infinite being of *love*. You are here to extend and express that love in all its varying forms. You are here to gain insight and experience from all of the events that you draw towards you, consciously and unconsciously - this occurs according to your thought processes and the choices that you make.

You may have noticed that you are hearing the same message over and over again? Yes, this message has been repeated many times because it is important for you to fully absorb the content of what is being said here ...

Have you noticed any synchronicities? What questions would you like answered? Do you have any thoughts regarding this way of viewing your life's journey?

Nerise Howes

Notes on this exercise

Start recording your dreams. Keep a notebook and a pen next to your bed. As soon as you wake up, write down everything you are able to remember from your dreams. This can be a valuable tool in becoming more aware and in tune with what is taking place within your subconscious mind. This exercise will also give you clues and insights into your life's current situations, fears, hopes and visions. Pay attention to recurring dreams, symbols or themes that are repeated in different ways.

Write it all down and be open to any insights that come to you during the day. The more you can begin to remember and consciously tune into your dream energy, the more will be revealed to you. Don't become obsessed with analysing each hidden meaning within every dream, simply be receptive to any insights that may arise as you focus on them. If nothing comes to mind, be patient and know that simply by acknowledging the dream you are creating a subconscious shift. Don't get lost in every detail of the dream, this will clutter your mind and create confusion. What is important for you to know will manifest itself to you in some form, in perfect time. Simply trust.

Nerise Howes

Notes on this exercise

FROM NOW ON I will see every mundane job as a way to grow spiritually.

Nothing you do in your life is unimportant or a waste of time. Be mindful today of every action. Take hold of each opportunity to put into practice your ability to choose your thoughts and actions. What you create now will affect the outcome of your future events and manifestations. Every moment in your life is a jewel to cherish. You do not know how long you have got here in this life, so make the *most* of it!

Driving to work, washing the dishes, changing nappies, negotiating a business deal or fixing the garden fence...these are golden opportunities among many others, where you can make each action a meditation and an expression of love or joy. It is a chance to *not* react from hurt or fear. It is the possibility of creating a "masterpiece' in the simplest of tasks ... this is all up to *you* and your power to *choose*!

The question to ask is, do you want to "suffer" and struggle through the day, wishing you were somewhere else instead? Or do you want to experience a sense of enjoyment, fun and happiness in everything you do?

If deciding the latter, then make a conscious decision to be present in each moment. This way you will never be a "victim", you will always be the conscious creator of your life. But with this comes the commitment of taking *full* responsibility for all that you think and do.

Nerise Howes

Notes on this exercise

Effortlessness. What does this word mean to you? How can you apply this feeling to your everyday activities and "mundane" tasks? What thought process would you need to change to make each activity a meditation of love, service and inner growth?

Nerise Howes

Notes on this exercise

Remember that where your attention goes, your energy will follow.

When you are able to hold an image in your mind's eye, you are essentially viewing a **possible** way or outcome for a specific situation to manifest in the physical realm. The more you **focus** on this image, the more energy you give it and the more likely it is that this image will start to "blossom" and take shape, as every vibration is created from a thought.

Let's go back to the very first exercise in this book, where you closed your eyes and visualised yourself as the person you would like to be.

Now, let's do this process again. Read through this first and then once you are familiar with relaxing deeply, do the exercise.

Find a comfortable position and a place where you won't be disturbed. Close your eyes and take three long, deep breaths. One ... two ... three. Imagine yourself sinking down...down into the ground and further... you feel really relaxed and you notice how all the tension dissipates from your body. Take your time, there is no rush. Every muscle in your body relaxes. You start to count down from twenty. Nineteen ... eighteen ... seventeen ... three ... two ... one ... zero. You see yourself. Where are you? Has anything changed? Do you look different? Do you act or feel different? Tune in to all your surroundings. Are you aware of any new visions, dreams, desires or insights? Take your time, observing yourself as you are. Notice how and in what way you may have changed, if at all.

Visualise how you effortlessly manifest all that you desire ... and how wonderfully happy and at peace you feel. The more details you can see, the better. Remain with this powerful image for a while and when you feel ready, start to count from zero to twenty. Zero ... one ... two ... three...seventeen ... eighteen ... nineteen ... twenty. Slowly become aware of the room again and feel your body. Gently pat your body to ground yourself back into the present.

Write down all your thoughts, feelings and images that came up for you during this exercise. Then simply trust and surrender to the unfolding of this visualisation in perfect time.

Notes on this exercise

I want you to meditate on, explore and think about the following words. What do they represent to you? What feelings, thoughts and images do they bring up physically, emotionally, mentally and spiritually?

Intuition

Insight

Memories

Perception

Timelessness

Repeat three times out loud:

I AM LOVE AND LIGHT DIVINE

THE CROWN CHAKRA

This chakra relates to connecting and unifying with the Divine Self and opening to infinite space and time.

Sanskrit name:	Sahasrara
Translation:	Thousandfold
Location:	The top of the head
Associated body parts:	The pituitary gland, the central nervous system and the brain
Colour:	Violet and White
Element:	Thought
Sound:	OM or EEE
Incense/oils:	Lavender, Frankincense, Rosewood
Crystals:	Clear Quartz, Diamond, White Tourmaline
Affirmation:	I am Love and Light Divine.

Remember to wear as much violet and/or white as possible this week, to integrate this vibration.

FROM NOW ON I make a conscious decision to live from *intention* … to live from my highest self.

Beautiful soul, *you* are an integral part of this world and this creation … there is only one *you*!

Being in service to others … offering your love in all that you say and do - herein lies great purpose, for the way in which you choose to express of yourself is completely unique.

You need to become aware of all your beautiful qualities. You need to start shining even more brightly than before. How will you do this?

Begin to *feel* that your life has indeed a special purpose. Integrate this understanding deep within and put it to practice every day. Remember that you have the opportunity to live your purpose, not just in the work that you choose to do, but also in every moment!

Your intention behind every decision and choice you make creates the reality you desire. Make your intention, to love.

Awareness. Awareness. Awareness. Through awareness comes the ability to be present in each moment, continuously. This then allows you to consciously choose your thoughts and actions. Therefore you can choose to live from intention in each moment. What will you choose to make *your* intention?

How do you choose to manifest your purpose? In what ways can you best express the essence of who you are and channel it in a unique way?

Nerise Howes

Notes on this exercise

FROM NOW ON I will always remember that I am never alone. I will ask for assistance from God or other beings of light, whenever I need guidance, knowing within that I *have* been heard. I will trust the process of my journey here and remember that I am *part* of the great web of life and therefore eternally one with all that is.

Start communicating with your spirit helpers. There are beings that are always ready to be of comfort, inspiration and guidance whenever you require it. It is important to *ask* for guidance, as you must remember that you have free will and choice. These beings are simply waiting to be of more assistance. They too, benefit from being in service as it gives them an opportunity to express their intention to love!

When asking for guidance remember to always be clear that you only want to connect with beings of light. You should always ask the being if they indeed do come from a higher vibrating space of love and light. Sometimes mischievous spirits or energies may want to come and play and create a little bit of confusion. Having your intention of love and light firmly within will attract the right kind of energy for you to be connecting with.

How can you connect more with your spirit guides? With which beings do you feel an affinity? Have you ever acknowledged that there may be other forms or beings existing in different realms other than what we can see? For example the angelic kingdom, ascended masters, elementals (fairies, elves, gnomes), inter- galactic beings et cetera.

Creation is infinite and therefore there are infinite different beings existing in infinite worlds and galaxies. There is a lot more information regarding other beings and other worlds available at present, for we are becoming more receptive and open to the idea that earth is a planet among many others. Beings from other realms also want to make contact with other planes of existence and therefore information is starting to come through different sources in various forms and ways. An example is through channelling, dreams and various sightings or visions of what is known as extraterrestrials.

It is not necessary to intellectually grasp the complexities of all creation. It would not be humanly possible at this point in time to understand it all at once, but simply remember that in essence we are all *one* in **Source**.

Find time to be still every day. Spend a little longer in your meditation session. Explore other meditation techniques (there are many wonderful books regarding this subject). Join a Yoga or meditation group.

Notes on this exercise

FROM NOW ON I will surround myself with things that add beauty and inspiration to my life.

In what way can you do this? Begin with your home. What could you do to make it a place you truly love to be, your sacred space and haven?

Become aware of the books that you read, the movies that you watch, the thoughts that you think and the discussions you may get involved with. Please note that I am *not* suggesting that you lead a sombre life void of all colour and variety or that you shy away from all that life has to offer ... not at all.

Be bold, expressive, free spirited, fearless, adventurous and all the wonderful qualities that you can be! Shine brightly... I am simply suggesting for you to become more *aware* of what you choose to include and surround yourself with in this life. This will help to shape and create a world for you that will accurately reflect the kind of energy you want to resonate with.

Explore and embrace life with an open heart and mind, without judgement. Simply be mindful that when you become discerning in your choice of what you want to include in your everyday life, then you are consciously deciding to become the master of your own destiny. Do you want to create a heaven here on earth? It is all a state of mind and choice. It is as simple as that.

Notes on this exercise

FROM NOW ON I will allow myself to *be* in the present moment. I will not dwell on the past, nor live in a projected future. Indeed I will have dreams, visions, desires and aspirations, but I will remain grounded into living each moment to its fullest potential. I am here, now, in the present.

This exercise is simply about bringing your awareness back to the eternal now. It is about valuing each precious moment and cherishing the time given to you here in this life. Therefore, make the most of where you are, right here, right now.

For today make this an exercise of consciously remaining present. Each time your mind wanders and you find yourself thinking about the past or longing for tomorrow to come ... bring yourself back to the present moment. You can ground yourself by doing something physical and active. This is how you will begin to cultivate a sense of timelessness.

Notes on this exercise

FROM NOW ON I will simplify my life. By reducing your wants and needs, what is really important in your life will become evident. By cultivating preferences but not attachments you will release the pain that always arises from loss.

How can you simplify your life? What does this mean to you?

Notes on this exercise

Nerise Howes

FROM NOW ON I will surrender my life to God. See yourself as an instrument in the hands of God. You are an Eternal Self serving the Eternal Self in all Its variations in form, here on earth. Consciously decide to allow more of God's energy to flow through you. What does this mean? Remembering that God is love ... allow yourself to become a vessel for extending this love, unconditionally, to everyone you meet and in everything you do. In what way can you surrender to this way of being?

Notes on this exercise

FROM NOW ON I will allow myself to *laugh*!

Being light-hearted and having a sense of humour- these are two magical attributes. Start to integrate these energies into your daily life and into your being. Begin today by seeing the funny side of things. Don't take yourself too seriously. You will begin to experience a wonderful sense of lightness from within. Give it a go, there is nothing to lose!

Notes on this exercise

FROM NOW ON I will think of myself as unlimited in every way…capable of creating *all* things. I, therefore, choose to create only that which brings the most happiness, the most beauty and the most *love*!

Feel these words deeply and integrate their meaning and energy.

Notes on this exercise

FROM NOW ON I will live as if I am an awakened Master or being. If you want to be close to God - be like Him, act like Him. Be the Buddha, be the Christ.

Always ask the question in your mind of what an ascended Master or awakened being would do in any given situation. By cultivating this awareness you will always know which path to take. Trust your intuition. Begin the day by tuning into living in this higher consciousness. It is a good idea to practice living in this state for short periods of time, for example ten minutes - then gradually extend the length of time as you are able to remain in this state.

Notes on this exercise

I want you to meditate on, explore and think about the following words. What do they represent to you? What feelings, images and thoughts do they bring up physically, emotionally, mentally and spiritually?

Awareness

Soul

Infinity

Inspiration

Consciousness

Unity

Reality

Repeat three times out loud:

I AM LOVE AND LIGHT DIVINE

PRAYER AND INVOCATION

(To be read out loud)

Great being of radiating Light,
Father and Mother to all of creation:
I give thanks to life in all its wondrous forms
and for being a part of all that is and was and shall be.
I acknowledge that I AM LOVE AND LIGHT DIVINE.
Knowing this, I set myself free.
I am free from all illusions of being separate.
For I am one with Thee, O great Spirit.
I therefore choose to live from a point of light within.
Loving all, embracing all and therefore, transcending all.
Thank you for this *awakening*
and for reminding me of this great truth.
I now make this my decree and my commitment;
To truly live from this understanding
FROM NOW ON…

It is time for you to write your own prayer or invocation. Don't over analyse what you write. Simply allow the words to flow.

My Prayer

Do you remember the very first question in this book? "What do you truly want?" I want you to think about this question once again. Has anything changed? Write down your thoughts and answers to this question. Take your time. Go within. Be still.

(Ask yourself at least three times)
"What do I truly want?"

Notes on this exercise

Final words ...

Beautiful Soul,

How would you like to be remembered?

Some day you will leave this earth plane and continue your journey elsewhere. What would you like to leave behind? What imprint of energy do you choose to be remembered by?

Think on this deeply ... for you are creating each precious moment. Therefore, FROM NOW ON create beautiful ones ... moments that shine and radiate love to all those who cross your path ... moments that allow you to live with a passion; fearless, courageous and effortless.

I would like you to write a paragraph on how you would like to be remembered when you decide to leave this earth plane, some day. This is not a sad or sombre exercise, quite the contrary. This is about celebrating your life and about taking it upon yourself to create something unique and something of value ... *today*. This will be that you may one day look back upon your life with great joy and inner satisfaction, knowing that you created the best life you could, with the knowledge and understanding you had at the time.

This will bring you much peace and you will happily continue your journey, having completed a lifetime filled with beautiful memories and indeed treasures of self transformation.

I (name)
Would like to be remembered for / as

I decided to include this last message I received, as it felt appropriate to remind myself that the *way* in which we tap into, share and receive information is of little importance. Trying to define how much of the content of this book was guided, inspired or put together from acquired knowledge is insignificant. It is important to trust our intuition in whatever way we receive or share information. If it resonates with us and feels true, simply embrace it. If the intention behind the words is coming from a place of love and light, then one would feel inspired and at peace. This has been my experience. The process of putting this workbook together has shown me in so many beautiful ways that our connection with ourselves, others, and with God is wonderfully and mysteriously intertwined. So here are the words I have surrendered to sharing as we come to the end of this workbook ...

The time has come for you to put all of your experience and insight into daily practice FROM NOW ON...

Please know that even though this book is coming to a close, this is far from being the end. In fact this is the start of a beautiful new beginning.

FROM NOW ON live with greater awareness. Practice extending love towards all beings.

If you are still wondering who I am ... I tell you this: I am the silent watcher. I am the wind, the sun, the moon and the stars. I am your brother, your sister and your eternal friend. I Am that I Am. I am LOVE and LIGHT DIVINE. This may come as a surprise to you, but I am also YOU! If this seems difficult to understand, simply remember that all life comes and returns to the same Source. We are all part of the ONE great Mind, Body and Spirit. Yet, we are unique, individual expressions of this energy.

There is only *one you*. Think deeply on these words...

I will always come when you call for me, as you are never alone. You are very much loved. Remember this.

Now you can pass this message on to someone else. Who do you know that may benefit from receiving this book? Trust your intuition.

But do not try and change anyone by trying to change his or her beliefs, as this will simply create more separation and confusion. Have the intention of becoming a shining example as a being of LOVE and LIGHT DIVINE. Remember the greatest gift that you can give the world is this - to remove *your own* "suffering" and to replace it with love.

You, most beautiful soul, were divinely drawn to finding this book. Therefore, find a way to integrate the message from within. The time is NOW! With this thought I wish you happiness, light, humility, joy and above all, I wish you all embracing LOVE and LIGHT DIVINE.

FROM NOW ON...

Useful Resources

Books:

Title: Wheels of life
Author: Judith Anodea
Publisher: Llewellyn Publication, 2003

Title: Eastern body, Western mind,
Author: Judith Anodea
Publisher: Celestial Arts Berkeley, 2004

Title: Meditation: The first and last freedom
Author: Osho
Publisher: Boxtree, 1995

Website

For more information: www.OneofSpirit.com
Chakradance: www.Chakradance.com